You Decide

Hannah is climbing on her favorite spinner at the park.

It's almost time to go home for dinner. "Five more minutes!" Mama calls out. That's just enough time for a little more fun.

Five minutes later, Mama says, "Let's go, Hannah! Grab your jacket and let's head to the car. Maybe we can see Uncle Zhenyu before he leaves our house."

Already? Hannah loves the spinner, but she also loves Uncle Zhenyu.

What will Hannah do?

★

Find her jacket and go to the car

Go to page 8

■

Ignore Mama and keep playing

Go to page 12

Hannah picks up her jacket and takes Mama's hand. They walk to the car together.

When they get there, Mama asks Hannah to climb into her car seat so she can get buckled in.

What will Hannah do?

Climb into her car seat

Go to page 20

Sit in the wrong seat

Go to page 34

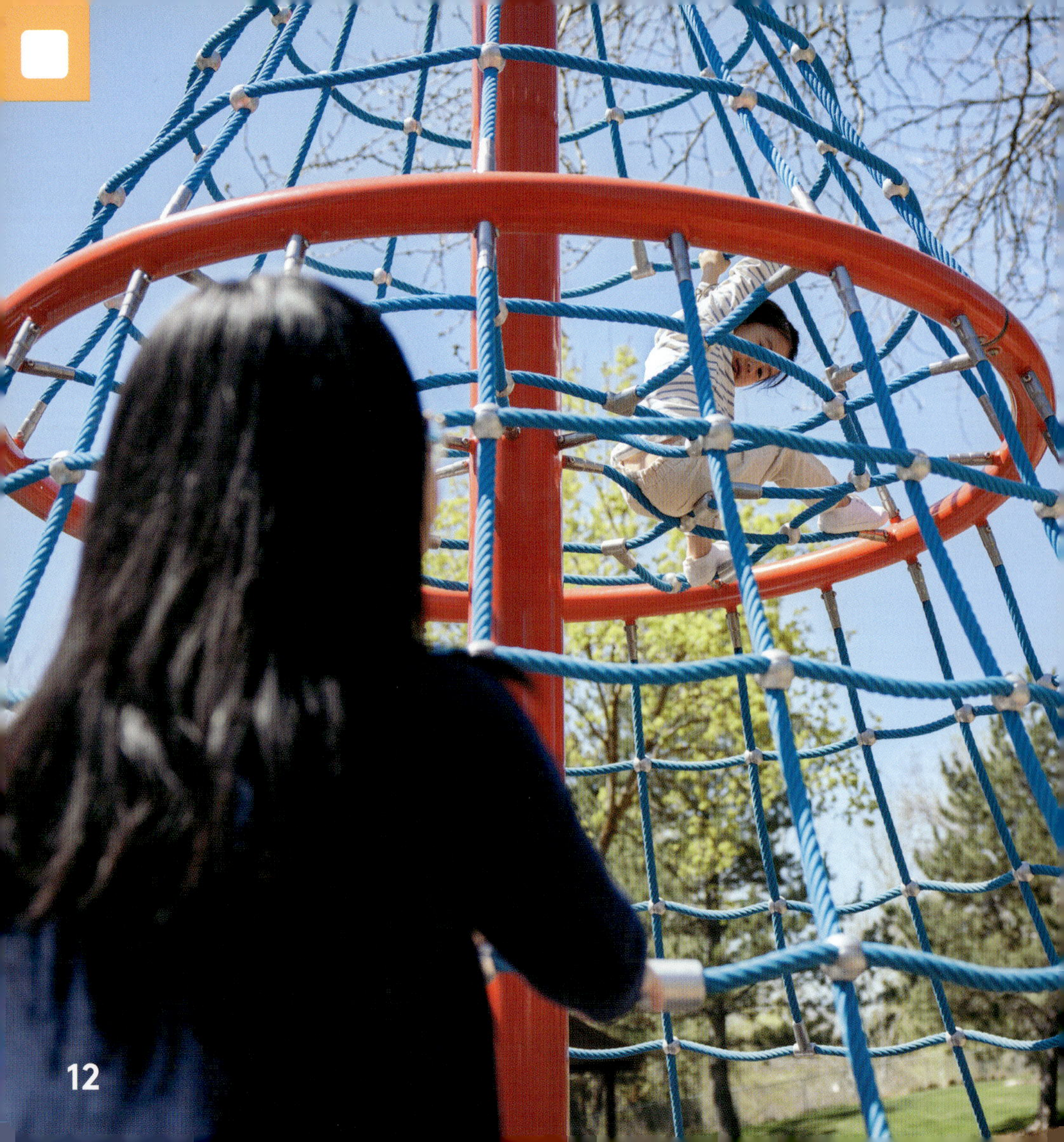

Hannah keeps climbing and spinning, again and again.

"I know it's hard to leave the park when you're having so much fun," says Mama, "but it's getting late. We need to go."

Hannah ignores her.

Hannah climbs down a little lower so she can spin really fast. Mama is right there, and she doesn't look happy.

"You can walk on your own, or I can pick you up and carry you."

Hannah still doesn't move, so Mama picks her up and carries her to the car. Hannah kicks and screams.

Mama asks Hannah to climb into her car seat. Hannah's cheeks are wet with tears, and she looks back at the park.

What will Hannah do?

Climb into her car seat

Go to page 42

Refuse to get into her car seat

Go to page 54

Hannah climbs into her car seat and spies something small and bright wedged below it. "My favorite toy!" she says, and holds it tight.

"Yay, you found it!" Mama says.
"We thought that toy was lost."

Mama buckles Hannah into
her seat.

rotecting our
lue Planet.
2516

As a recycling truck passes through the park, Hannah calls out, "Look, I found my toy car!"

"Wow!" says the truck driver. "How cool!"

"That was fun! Do you want to pick a song to listen to?" Mama asks.

Hannah chooses her favorite song, and dances in her car seat the whole way home.

Uncle Zhenyu is still at their house when they get there.

"Can we fly paper airplanes together?" Hannah asks. That's her favorite thing to do with Uncle Zhenyu.

Hannah and Uncle Zhenyu throw their paper airplanes in the yard.

They watch the planes twist and twirl through the air before landing softly on the grass.

Uncle Zhenyu gets ready to go.

"I'm so glad we got to fly paper airplanes together," he says.

"Me too," says Hannah. "I can't wait to do it again."

The End

Hannah climbs onto her older sister's booster seat. She's not old enough to ride in it yet, but it makes her feel big.

Mama sighs. "I need you to sit in your own car seat, please."

Hannah keeps playing.

"Please climb in, my love, so we can get going," Mama says.

Hannah ignores her. She's having fun playing Big Kid.

"I'm going to pick you up now, so I can buckle you in safely," Mama says.

She lifts Hannah out of the booster and buckles her into her own car seat. Hannah kicks and cries.

2516
Protecting our
Blue Planet.
CAUTION
VEHICLE STOPS AND BACKS FREQUENTLY

"Can I pick a song?" Hannah asks between deep breaths.

"I need quiet right now, Hannah," Mama answers.

Behind them, a recycling truck rounds the corner, but Hannah doesn't see it.

Go to page 48

Hannah spots her favorite toy car, which she thought she had lost. She picks it up and the tears start to slow down.

She takes a deep breath and climbs straight into her car seat, buckling the top part by herself. Mama helps with the tricky bottom part.

A recycling truck is picking up bins from the park.

Hannah loves the sounds it makes, and how its metal arm goes up high above the ground. Hannah waves to the drivers, but they don't see her.

McNeilus
2516

"Do you want to pick a song?" Mama asks.

Hannah chooses a lullaby, and falls asleep on the short drive home.

When they get home, Uncle Zhenyu is just walking out the door. Hannah runs up to him and jumps into his arms.

"My Hannah Banana!" Uncle Zhenyu says. "I was just about to leave."

"Can we make paper airplanes?" Hannah asks.

"Sorry, Hannah. I have to be somewhere in a few minutes. We'll have to make paper airplanes next time."

Hannah's shoulders slump. "Okay," she sighs.

Uncle Zhenyu waves goodbye.

"I can tell you wanted more time with Uncle Zhenyu," says Mama.

"Yes," Hannah says. "Next time, I'm going to make different choices."

The End

Hannah doesn’t want to get into her car seat. She sits down on the sidewalk.

Mama lets out a long breath. "We have to go or we’ll miss Uncle Zhenyu," she says.

Hannah crosses her arms.

"Can you climb in on your own,
or shall I help you?"

Hannah keeps her arms crossed.

Mama sits down next to her.

Finally, after a long time, Mama picks Hannah up.

Hannah's body is floppy like a noodle, and she doesn't help Mama at all.

She sees her favorite toy stuck under the seat, but she can't reach it.

When they get home, Hannah looks around for her uncle, but she doesn’t see him.

"Where’s Uncle Zhenyu?" she asks Mama.

"He must have gone home."

"I can see that you're feeling sad," Mama says. "This was a hard afternoon for you, but mistakes help us learn and choose differently next time."

Hannah gives Mama a hug.
It helps to remember there's always a next time.

The End